G
Eas
Pu_ ..aiks

David Weller

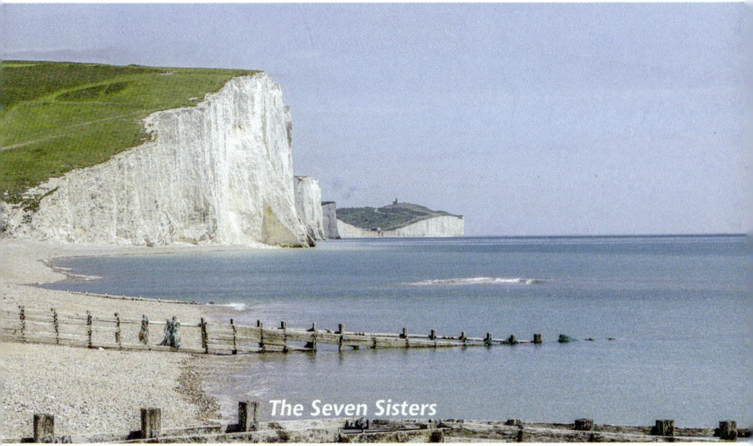

The Seven Sisters

COUNTRYSIDE BOOKS
NEWBURY BERKSHIRE

First published 2018
Text © 2018 David Weller

All rights reserved. No part of this publication may be reproduced, stored in a retrieval system, or transmitted by any means, electronic, mechanical, photocopying, recording or otherwise, without the prior written permission of the copyright holder and publishers.

The right of David Weller to be identified as the author of this work has been asserted by him in accordance with the Copyright, Designs, and Patents Act 1988.

COUNTRYSIDE BOOKS
3 Catherine Road
Newbury, Berkshire

To view our complete range of books,
please visit us at
www.countrysidebooks.co.uk

ISBN 978 1 84674 365 8

Designed by KT Designs, St Helens
Produced through The Letterworks Ltd., Reading
Typeset by KT Designs, St Helens
Printed in Poland

Introduction

East Sussex has an extraordinarily diverse landscape, ranging from the flatlands of the Pevensey Levels to the heights of Beachy Head and across the magnificent Seven Sisters Country Park. Just inland from here, the county boasts a section of the newly formed South Downs National Park, while to the north of that lies the Weald, which has been described as a quintessentially medieval landscape.

Dotted around this lovely panorama are the county's villages and small towns, each home to a good pub, many of them dating back centuries. All of these circular routes start and finish at a pub, and I have ensured that there is always parking available, whether in the pub car park or close by. Out of courtesy, it is always best to ask first if you are parking in the pub car park.

Whether you are out walking on a hot summer's day, when you seek shade under a colourful umbrella in a sunny pub garden, or on a

The Horse & Groom, Rushlake Green

Guide to East Sussex Pub Walks

chilly winter's day, with your chair pulled up to a warming log fire in an ancient inglenook fireplace, there will always be a hearty pub meal to enjoy.

While my instructions and sketch maps will get you around these circuits easily, I would always recommend you take the appropriate OS map for a better overview of the route. Another recommendation I would make is to wear good walking boots or shoes that will give support on uneven or slippery ground.

Here's to happy walking!

David Weller

Publisher's Note

We hope that you obtain considerable enjoyment from this book: great care has been taken in its preparation. However, changes of landlord and actual pub closures are sadly not uncommon. Likewise, although at the time of publication all routes followed public rights of way or permitted paths, diversion orders can be made and permissions withdrawn.

In order to assist in navigation to the start point of the walk, we have included the nearest postcode, although of course a postcode cannot always deliver you to a precise starting point, especially in rural areas.

We cannot, of course, be held responsible for such diversion orders or any inaccuracies in the text which result from these or any other changes to the routes, nor any damage which might result from walkers trespassing on private property. We are anxious, though, that all details covering the walks and the pubs are kept up to date, and would therefore welcome information from readers which would be relevant to future editions.

The simple sketch maps that accompany the walks in this book are based on notes made by the author whilst surveying the routes on the ground. They are designed to show you how to reach the start and to point out the main features of the overall circuit, and they contain a progression of numbers that relate to the paragraphs of the text.

However, for the benefit of a proper map, we do recommend that you purchase the relevant Ordnance Survey sheet covering your walk. Ordnance Survey maps are widely available, especially through booksellers and local newsagents.

A farm track along the way

1 Ditchling
3¾ miles (6 km)

WALK HIGHLIGHTS
This good, level, rural walk leaves the village by following well-marked paths across fields to meet the manicured grounds of Mid Sussex Golf Club. From here, the way crosses more fields to reach farm tracks offering far-reaching views to the South Downs as the route returns to Ditchling. Those with alektorophobia should be aware that the route passes through a couple of fields containing free-range chickens.

THE PUB
The Bull, BN6 8TA
☎ 01273 843147 www.thebullditchling.com

Guide to East Sussex Pub Walks

HOW TO GET THERE AND PARKING: Ditchling is about a mile east of Hassocks, and lies at the crossroads of the B2116 and B2112. The pub is at the crossroads itself. Park in the pub car park in Lewes Road (B2116) with permission, or in the village hall's free car park opposite. **Sat nav** BN6 8TA.

MAP: OS Explorer OL11 Brighton & Hove. **Grid ref** TQ 326151.

THE WALK

1. With your back to the pub car park, go left along the road before forking left on a drive named the **Fieldway**. At its end, continue on a path to meet a road. Cross into **Farm Lane** opposite, and in 25 metres, go left on a signed path. Follow the path, crossing some unique stiles along the way to meet a fenced field containing free-range chickens.

2. Pass through a gate into the field, and go straight across to another gate at the far side, being careful not to let any chickens escape. Cross a stile, and go diagonally right over a farm drive and through a gate to enter the next field. At the far side, pass through a squeeze stile, and go ahead to a marker post. Pass this, and go through a gate at the far side to enter woodland, meeting a footbridge and a stile at a field edge.

3. Turn right along the field edge, and cross a stile in the corner. Go ahead through the next field, and cross a stile beside a tree in the far hedgerow. Go diagonally left to a gate in the distance, and cross a stile beside it to meet a road.

4. Cross to a stile opposite, and go diagonally left through a field. At the far side, continue through scrub to meet a track at a golf course. Turn left; you will soon pass to the right of a car park. Press on along the path, and when you are opposite the clubhouse, go left on a path that bends right around a putting green to meet a directional post.

6

Ditchling 1

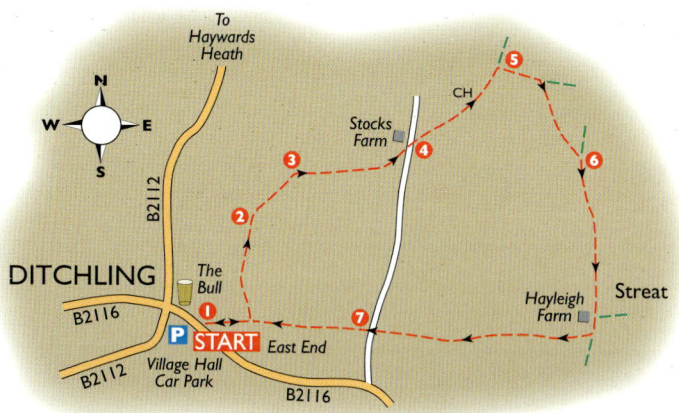

5 Turn right here, and cross the golf course, following the marker posts. As you leave the golf course, you meet a bridge on your right. Cross this, and go diagonally left over a field to a gate in the corner. Continue through the next field to a stile in the hedgerow to the left of a house; cross it to meet a track.

6 Turn right along the track, which later passes a couple of cottages. Ignore a bridleway to the left, but soon after, turn right along a farm drive by a duck pond. Follow this drive through open fields until it ends at a road.

7 Cross to a signed path opposite, and keep ahead as it passes a recreation ground and a cricket pitch. Soon, you rejoin your outward path; continue ahead to meet the pub and the end of this good circuit.

PLACES OF INTEREST NEARBY
Ditchling Museum of Art + Craft (www.ditchlingmuseumartcraft.org.uk) specializes in showcasing the work of the artists and craftspeople that made the village a creative hub in the 20th century. The museum is off the B2116, west of the crossroads. BN6 8SP.

The path to Falmer Bottom

2 Kingston near Lewes

4¾ miles (7.6 km)

WALK HIGHLIGHTS

This easy-to-follow, energetic walk climbs 350 feet to the top of the South Downs, where the rewards are stunning panoramic views over the countryside. After following the South Downs Way for a short distance, the route descends through Castle Hill Nature Reserve, a springtime delight. Continuing through peaceful Falmer Bottom, the route makes a second, somewhat easier climb, before descending steeply to return to the Juggs.

THE PUB
The Juggs, BN7 3NT
☎ 01273 472523 www.thejuggs.co.uk

THE WALK

1 With your back to the pub, turn right along **The Street** to meet **St Pancras church**. At the end of the churchyard, turn right on a path.

Kingston near Lewes

HOW TO GET THERE AND PARKING: Kingston near Lewes is signed off the A27 at a roundabout just south of Lewes. Follow a lane into the village, and at a left bend, turn right into The Street to meet the pub. Park at the pub with permission, or by the roadside. **Sat nav** BN7 3NT.

MAP: OS Explorer OL11 Brighton & Hove. **Grid ref** TQ 393082.

Follow the path where it turns left and passes some tennis courts. At its end, go ahead, pass a modern pavilion, and keep ahead along a private road. At the road's end, press on along a rising tarmac path to meet a crossing byway.

Turn left on the chalky byway, which leads to the escarpment. Along the way, ignore a left fork, and keep to the byway as it climbs to the top of the **Downs**. At the top, pass through a gate, and bear left towards a fence line, which you should follow until you meet **Castle Hill National Nature Reserve** on your left.

Turn left here on a downhill path, and exit via a gate at its end. Turn left alongside a field, and continue until a gate is finally reached. Pass through this gate, and go towards a further gate beside some farm buildings, but do not go through it.

Turn hard left up a short grassy rise to a gate at a field edge. Go ahead through this field and the next two fields on a sometimes indistinct path that follows the valley floor and finally brings you to a gate beside a farm building.

The Juggs

Guide to East Sussex Pub Walks

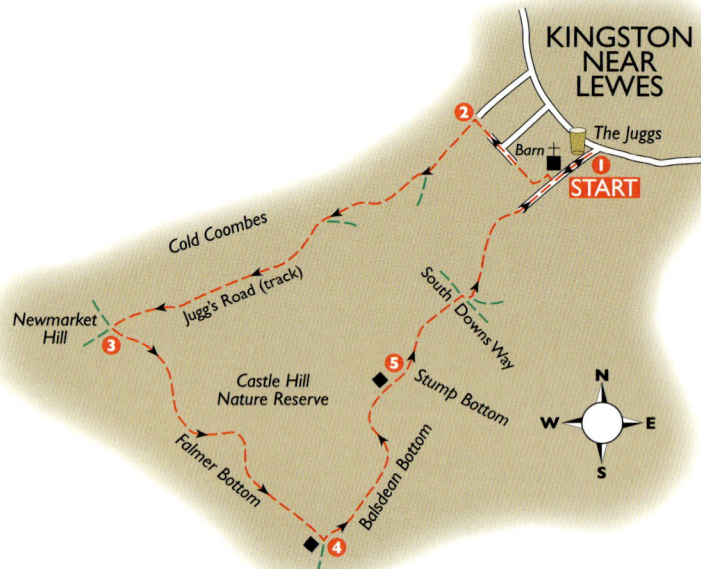

5 Press on, and follow a stony track that rises to the top of the Downs. At the top, ignore the signed **South Downs Way**, and go ahead on a bridleway. In 40 metres, turn left on a narrow path that goes downhill – steeply in parts – and finally ends at The Street, where you should go ahead to return to The Juggs.

PLACES OF INTEREST NEARBY
Anne of Cleves House Museum (www.sussexpast.co.uk/properties-to-discover/anne-of-cleves-house) is in nearby Lewes. This impressive 15th-century Wealden hall house was given to Anne as part of her divorce settlement by Henry VIII, and displays authentically furnished rooms and a garden with traditional Tudor planting. BN7 1JA.

Forest Way offers easy walking

3 Forest Row
3¼ miles (5.2 km)

WALK HIGHLIGHTS
After leaving the bustling village centre, this route very quickly immerses you in a rustic setting, where field paths and cart tracks will lead you beside fields to Horseshoe Farm. From here, the route turns to meet with the Forest Way; once a railway line, this charming tree-lined track offers easy walking through the countryside as it heads back to the village.

THE PUB
Brambletye Hotel, RH18 5EZ
☎ 01342 824144 www.brambletyehotel.co.uk

THE WALK
1 With your back to the hotel, go right for 50 metres, and turn right on a signed path between shops. Go ahead through a parking area and along a shingle path. Cross a bridge, and keep to the well-trodden path to

Guide to East Sussex Pub Walks

HOW TO GET THERE AND PARKING: The hotel is on the A22 at Forest Row, towards the northern end of the village. Park at the hotel with permission, by the roadside, or at one of the two free village car parks. **Sat nav** RH18 5EZ.

MAP: OS Explorer 135 Ashdown Forest. **Grid ref** TQ 424353.

reach a stile. Enter a field, and continue ahead towards a house at the far side.

2 At the corner of the field, cross a stile, and keep ahead to a second stile beside a barn. Cross it, and then cross another stile at the end of the building to meet a house. Turn right on an enclosed path, and cross a stile ahead. Cross a second stile, and go ahead to pass through a pedestrian gate. Go diagonally left, and cross a stile in the hedgerow.

3 Go ahead on a grassy path to meet a crossing bridleway. Turn right; cross a bridge and follow the bridleway as it passes a garden and meets a junction of tracks. Turn left along the track, which soon goes around a house and garden. Keep to the track until it ends by a large barn.

4 Here, press on ahead on a cart track that soon becomes enclosed. Ignore a path on your left, and continue on the cart track until it finally ends. Go ahead through a hedgerow, and cross the centre of a field, passing under some power cables. At the far side, continue on an enclosed path to the left of a gap in the tree line.

5 The path brings you to the drive of **Horseshoe Farm**. Turn right along the drive. After a rise, you will meet a bridge parapet; turn immediately right here on a descending path to meet the **Forest Way**, a defunct railway line between East Grinstead and Forest Row.

6 Go ahead along this wonderful

Forest Row 3

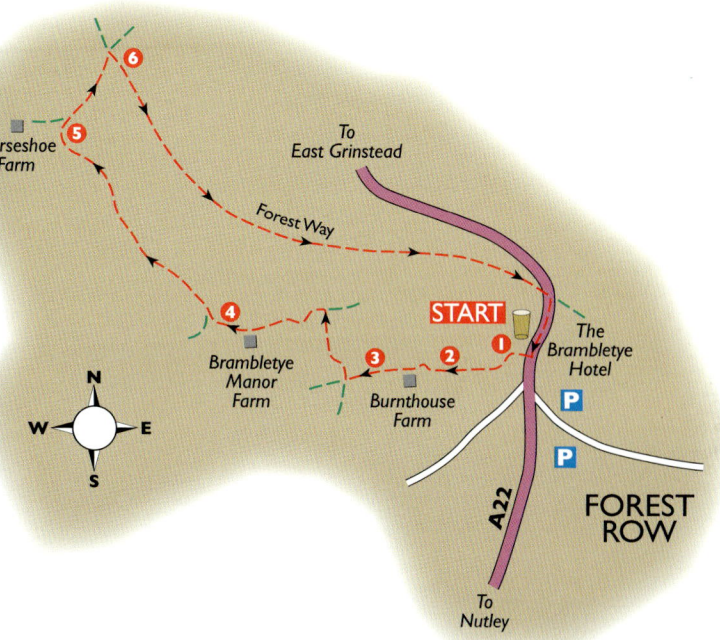

track – which is shared with cyclists – for just over 1¼ miles, until it ends at some pedestrian traffic lights on the A22. Do not cross the road. Instead, turn right along the pavement; very soon, you will reach the hotel.

PLACES OF INTEREST NEARBY
Standen House and Garden (www.nationaltrust.org.uk/standen-house-and-garden) was acquired by the National Trust in 1972; since then, this Grade I listed Arts and Crafts house has been open to the public. RH19 4NE.

The picturesque River Ouse

4 Isfield
3¼ miles (5.2 km)

WALK HIGHLIGHTS
This level route passes through quiet, rural countryside as it makes its way to the turning point by the Anchor Inn, idyllically situated on the bank of the River Ouse. You can stop here for refreshment or even hire a canoe during the summer months to enjoy the pleasures of this picturesque river. The route then follows the riverbank for some way before joining your outward path. Some paths can become muddy during winter.

THE PUB
The Laughing Fish, TN22 5XB
☎ 01825 750349   www.thelaughingfish.co.uk

THE WALK
1 With your back to the pub, turn right along the road. 50 metres after passing **Culpeper Close**, turn left on a bridleway along a private lane.

Isfield 4

HOW TO GET THERE AND PARKING: Isfield is signed from the A26, 5 miles north of Lewes. Turn into Station Road to find the pub, which is next to the old railway station. Park at the pub with permission or at the roadside. **Sat nav** TN22 5XB.

MAP: OS Explorer OL25 Eastbourne & Beachy Head. **Grid ref** TQ 451171.

Later, ignore a left fork, and continue, soon meeting the **River Ouse** at **White Bridge**. Cross the bridge, and go left through a pedestrian gate to enter a large field. Go diagonally half-left, and follow a grassy path to the far side.

Pass through a gate, cross a bridge, and turn left on a well-trodden path. Cross a stile, and follow a grassy path that soon passes to the right of a Second World War pillbox. Now, go ahead on a wide, grassy track between hedgerows, which eventually ends at **Anchor Lane**.

Guide to East Sussex Pub Walks

The Laughing Fish

❸ Turn left along the lane to meet the **Anchor Inn**. Pass the pub, cross a bridge, and turn left through a kissing gate to join the **Sussex Ouse Valley Way** path. The indistinct path now follows the riverbank through several scenic fields, passing under a disused railway bridge along the way. The path eventually returns you to White Bridge and the private lane. Turn right here, and retrace your steps back to the Laughing Fish.

PLACES OF INTEREST NEARBY
The Lavender Line (www.lavender-line.co.uk) is a preserved steam railway run by volunteers; its Victorian station and signal box are right next door to the pub. The two-mile round trip through the Wealden countryside from Isfield offers the sights and sounds of a past era. Check for opening times. TN22 5XB.

A farm drive walked on the route

5 Fletching
3¼ miles (5.2 km)

WALK HIGHLIGHTS
This gently undulating route offers glorious panoramic views over the surrounding countryside, crossing fields as it heads for the hamlet of Down Street. Turning here along a quiet country lane, the route meets Mallingdown Farm, passing the farmhouse as the way heads easily back across fields to Fletching.

THE PUB
The Griffin Inn, TN22 3SS
☎ 01825 722890 www.thegriffininn.co.uk

THE WALK
1. With your back to the pub, cross the road, and turn right along the pavement, which brings you to a church. Turn left alongside a cottage

Guide to East Sussex Pub Walks

HOW TO GET THERE AND PARKING: Fletching is signed from the A22 at Nutley and from the A272 at Piltdown, west of Uckfield. Park at the pub with permission or in the free village car park opposite. **Sat nav** TN22 3SS.

MAP: OS Explorer 135 Ashdown Forest. **Grid ref** TQ 428236.

wall before continuing to the far end of the graveyard. Turn left to meet and pass through a kissing gate.

2 Ignore a path to your right, and go ahead diagonally through a large field to a stile in the corner. Go ahead over the next field, and cross a stile by some trees to meet a cart track. Turn right, and when the track ends at a gate, cross a stile beside it, and continue diagonally right to meet and cross a stile at the edge of some woodland.

3 Go through a gully, and cross a footbridge and a stile to enter a field. Now, go diagonally right to a stile, which you should cross to enter the next field. Go ahead, pass through a gap in the hedgerow at the far side, and bear right towards some trees.

4 Pass through a squeeze stile, cross a bridge, and go ahead along the left side of a barn. Pass through a gate, and continue along a drive to a second gate to meet a quiet lane. Turn right along the lane to arrive at a T-junction.

5 Turn right here, and continue for ¾ mile. Soon after passing **Mallingdown Farm** entrance on your right, turn right on a driveway that brings you to a gate. Go ahead along the drive; pass the front of the farmhouse and **Mallingdown Oast**.

6 Press on along a short cart track and then the left side of a field. Cross a stile at the field end, and then a second stile, to continue on a path between hedgerows; when you meet a field, continue along its left edge, and cross a stile at the far left corner.

7 Cross the stile, turn right along the field edge, and cross a stile on your right. Turn left, and continue towards a stile and a bridge on your left.

Fletching

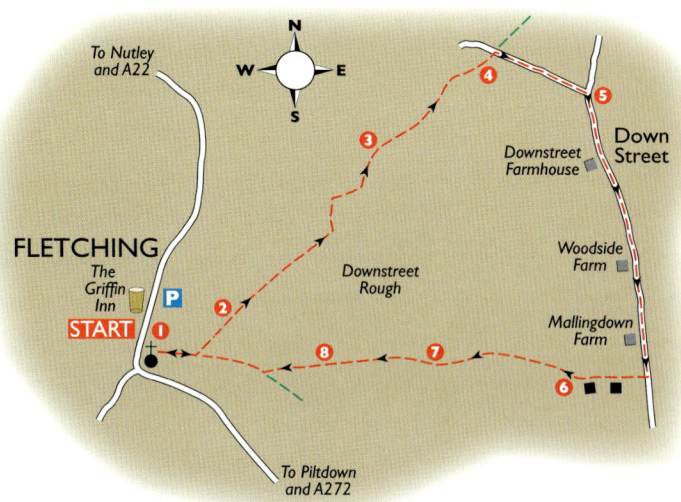

Cross the bridge, and press on to the top of the hill. Cross a stile in the hedgerow on the skyline ahead.

8 Go diagonally half-left across the field to meet and cross a stile in the hedgerow. Turn right along a rough track, and where it bends left, go ahead through a gate. Now go ahead, keeping to the right of a large barn and some silos to rejoin your outward path by the kissing gate in the graveyard boundary; from here, you can retrace your steps back to the pub.

PLACES OF INTEREST NEARBY
Sheffield Park and Garden (www.nationaltrust.org.uk/sheffield-park-and-garden), a landscaped garden originally laid out in the 18th century by Capability Brown, is off the A275, about 2 miles west of Fletching. TN22 3QX.

Beanstalk Tea Garden

6 Firle
4 miles / 6.4 km

WALK HIGHLIGHTS
This undulating circuit stays within the Firle Estate, which lies below the South Downs. After leaving the village, the way passes through pristine parkland before crossing scenic fields to reach Charleston Farmhouse, the spiritual home of the Bloomsbury Group. The circuit then meets with and follows a wonderful byway that leads easily back to the pretty village, passing Beanstalk, a unique tea garden, along the way.

THE PUB
The Ram Inn, BN8 6NS
☎ 01273 858222 www.raminn.co.uk

Firle 6

HOW TO GET THERE AND PARKING: Firle is off the A27, 4 miles west of the Drusillas Park roundabout. Keep ahead by the entrance to Firle Place, and soon afterwards, follow the road left into the village to park at the free village car park. **Sat nav** BN8 6NS.

MAP: OS Explorer OL25 Eastbourne & Beachy Head. **Grid ref** TQ 468074.

THE WALK

1 With your back to the pub, go left along the village street, passing a small memorial hall along the way. At the village stores, go left on a track, and pass some pretty cottage gardens. The track continues through parkland, where it soon crosses a tarmac drive.

2 Cross the drive, and now gradually begin to leave the track by going diagonally right across the grass to a footpath marker post to the right of some trees. From here, go ahead, and pass a second marker post to reach a gate with two cottages beyond it.

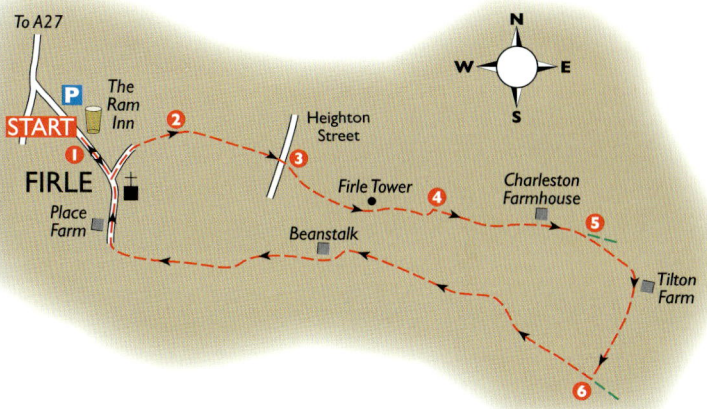

Guide to East Sussex Pub Walks

❸ Pass through the gate, and go ahead on a signed bridleway between the cottages. Follow the narrow bridleway; soon it goes diagonally right uphill towards woodland. Pass through a ribbon of woodland, cross a track, and press on ahead through a large arable field.

❹ Maintain your direction on the bridleway as it passes through fields and brings you to **Charleston Farmhouse**. Pass the house, and continue along the drive to a T-junction.

❺ Turn right here along another drive. After passing between fields, follow the drive to the right and pass by some barns. It soon becomes a cart track and continues towards the escarpment of the **Downs**, where it ends at a T-junction with a byway.

❻ Turn right here, and remain on this old byway for 1½ miles until it finally ends back at the village street in **Firle**. Along the way, the track passes **Beanstalk**, a wonderfully unique tea garden. Check for opening times; you can call on 01273 858906.

PLACES OF INTEREST NEARBY
Charleston Farmhouse (www.charleston.org.uk) is signed off the A27, two miles east of the Firle turning. In the first half of the 20th century, this farmhouse was home to several of the artists who became known as the Bloomsbury Group. Check for opening times. BN8 6LL.

The Wealden views are stunning

7 Hartfield

4½ miles (7.2 km)

WALK HIGHLIGHTS

This great country walk begins in Hartfield's quaint High Street, before heading off along the trackbed of a defunct railway. After turning north through woodland, it meets its highest point, where there are fine Wealden views across the Medway Valley. The return route descends through lovely pastoral fields to rejoin the old railway trackbed, which now forms a lovely linear country park called the Forest Way.

THE PUB
The Anchor Inn, TN7 4AG
☎ 01892 770424 www.anchorhartfield.com

Guide to East Sussex Pub Walks

HOW TO GET THERE AND PARKING: Hartfield is on the B2110, 4 miles east of the A22 at Forest Row. The Anchor Inn is on the corner of Church Street and the High Street. There is parking at the pub for customers, or you can park by the roadside. **Sat nav** TN7 4AG.

MAP: OS Explorer 135 Ashdown Forest. **Grid ref** TQ 478357.

THE WALK

1 With your back to the pub, turn right along the **High Street**. Soon, turn left into **Edenbridge Road**. Pass a car park entrance on your right, and go ahead on a path beside it to reach the old railway track. Turn left under a bridge, and continue along the track. Just before a second bridge, fork right up a slope to a bridleway. Bear right along the bridleway, and cross the **River Medway**. Keep to the rising bridleway to meet a single-track farm road.

2 Turn left along the farm road, and in ¼ mile, look out for a stile on your left with another stile hidden in the hedgerow opposite, on your right. Cross the stile on your right, and follow a well-trodden path diagonally left through an arable field to its end at a campsite at **St Ives Farm West**.

3 Go ahead over a grassy area to meet a track with a pond beyond it. Follow the track to the right, and soon cross a small grassy area to meet and cross a stile in the corner of a field. Press on along the right side of the field. Ignore a gate and path on your right along the way, and continue to the end of the field.

4 Turn left here, with a tree line on your right, and go downhill, soon bearing rightwards around an outcrop of woodland, before following the grassy path as it swings left to meet a field cart track.

5 Turn right along this cart track, and in 80 metres, before you meet the field gates, turn left on a signed footpath that descends down the field edge. Pass through a tree line, and continue ahead alongside the next field.

6 At the field end, pass through a gap in the hedgerow, ignore the paths

Hartfield 7

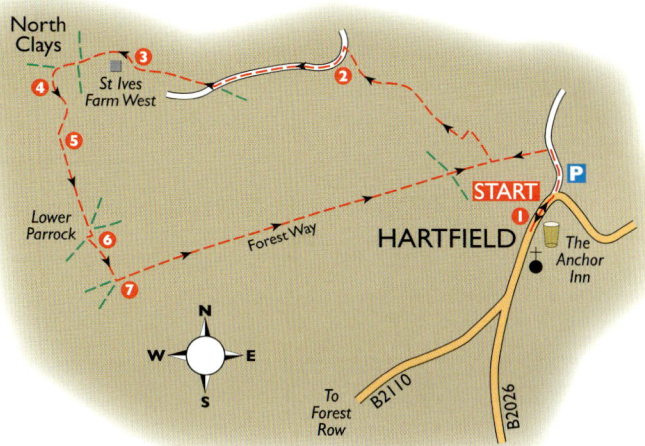

signed to the left and right, and go ahead on a narrow path. The path soon bends right and passes through a kissing gate. Go ahead over a strip of grass to meet the driveway of an isolated house. Turn left along the drive, and go over the River Medway; shortly, you will meet the **Forest Way**, which crosses the drive.

7 Turn left along the **Forest Way**, where 1¼ miles of easy walking will return you to Edenbridge Road, from where you should retrace your steps. Be aware that the track is shared with cyclists.

PLACES OF INTEREST NEARBY
Groombridge Place (www.groombridgeplace.com) has a variety of formal gardens that include knot, oriental, secret and – strangely – a drunken garden. From Hartfield, continue on the B2110 east towards Groombridge, pass through the village, and Groombridge Place is on the left after ¼ mile. TN3 9QG.

Panoramic views across Ashdown Forest

8 Fairwarp

3¾ miles (6 km)

WALK HIGHLIGHTS
This is an easy-to-follow circuit along wide tracks through the scenic landscape of Ashdown Forest, which was a deer-hunting forest in Norman times. It is the largest public open space in south-east England, and is at the very heart of the High Weald Area of Outstanding Natural Beauty. The panoramic views southward across the forest towards the South Downs are quite stunning.

THE PUB
The Foresters Arms, TN22 3BP
☎ 01825 712808   www.theforestersfairwarp.com

THE WALK

1 From the pub, walk back towards the B2026. 35 metres after passing the village green, turn right on a track, passing by **Spinners and Spinners Cottage**. Continue along the track, ignoring a path to your left. Soon, when the track bends right, go ahead on a woodland path, and pass the rear of **Christ Church**.

Fairwarp 8

HOW TO GET THERE AND PARKING: Fairwarp village is signed off the B2026, about 5¼ miles north of Uckfield. You reach the pub 300 metres after the turning. There is parking at the pub for customers, or you can park by the roadside. **Sat nav** TN22 3BP.

MAP: OS Explorer 135 Ashdown Forest. **Grid ref** TQ 468266.

2 At a crossing cart track, turn left to meet the B2026. Cross the road, and continue along the drive to **Spring Garden Farm**. Follow this gravel track as it leads you through woodland and passes the entrance gate of the farm.

3 Soon, at a junction of tracks, keep ahead. In 50 metres, ignore both a right fork and, soon afterwards, a left fork. Keep ahead, and before long, the track descends into a valley, where a woodland stream is crossed via a small planked bridge on your right.

4 The route maintains the same direction over a second small bridge, and continues up the slope opposite, where you should press on towards the brow of the hill.

5 At the brow of the hill, follow the broad track to the right; ignore the track to your left and another track ahead.

6 Press on uphill until you meet a T-junction by a large picnic area with a car park beyond it. Turn right here, follow the track along the top of the ridge, and pass by a second car park and an information board. Keep ahead, and continue on a wide, rising, curving grassy track.

7 At the foot of a dip, ignore a left fork, and keep to the main track, from which you will see a house ahead of you in the trees. When you are nearing the house, remain on the track as it bends leftwards. Soon, cross a drive leading to the house, and continue ahead. Cross a second drive, and again continue ahead.

8 Later, ignore a broad, grassy crossing track, and continue ahead to reach a wide, gravel crossing track 80 metres further on. This is the **Spring Garden Farm** track you walked earlier. Turn left, cross the B2026, and

Guide to East Sussex Pub Walks

go ahead to a junction of paths, where you should turn right and retrace your steps back to the pub.

PLACES OF INTEREST NEARBY

Ashdown Forest Llama Park (www.llamapark.co.uk) is home to a host of animals, including alpacas, reindeer, Jacob sheep, donkeys and pigs, as well as the llamas. The park is about 4 miles north-west of Fairwarp on the A22, at Wych Cross. RH18 5JN.

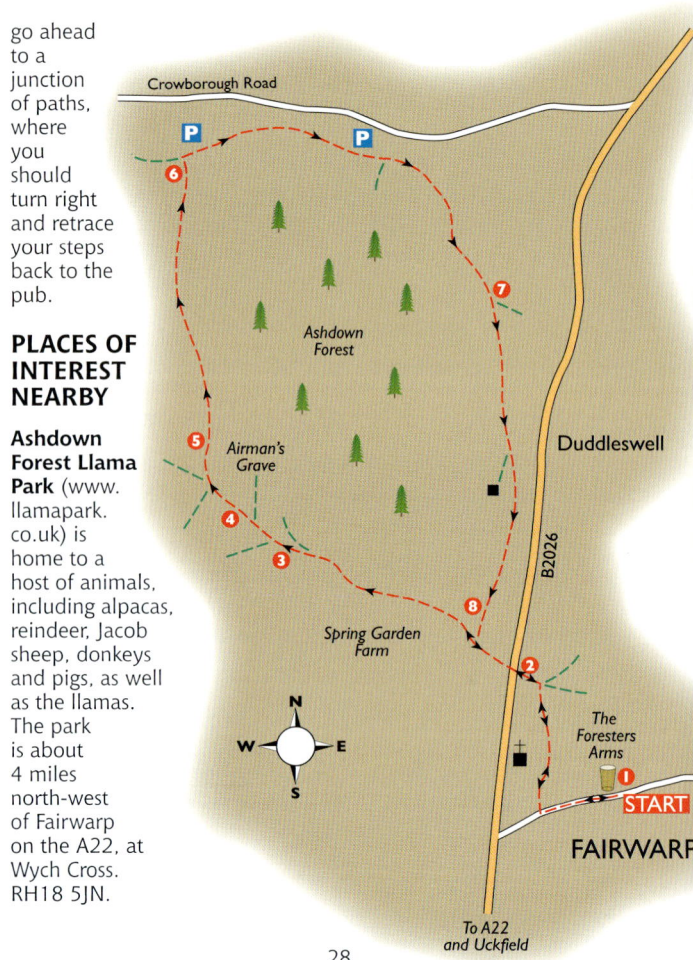

The cliff top path entering Hope Gap

9 Exceat

4¼ miles (6.8 km)

WALK HIGHLIGHTS

This lovely walk begins by passing through rising fields to reach a quiet lane; from here, it is a fairly short climb to the clifftop path at Seaford Head. The path offers stunning views across a seascape said to be the best in southern England. Leaving the coast, the route drops down into the Cuckmere Valley, and returns easily to the pub.

THE PUB
The Cuckmere Inn, BN25 4AB
☎ 01323 892247 www.vintageinn.co.uk

Guide to East Sussex Pub Walks

HOW TO GET THERE AND PARKING: The pub is on the A259 Eastbourne Road at the western end of Exceat Bridge, a mile east of Seaford. Park in one of the pub car parks. There is alternative parking (pay and display) ¼ mile eastwards at Exceat, across the causeway. **Sat nav** BN25 4AB.

MAP: OS Explorer OL25 Eastbourne & Beachy Head. **Grid ref** TV 514993.

THE WALK

1 Leave the car park via a gate at the end furthest from the road, and follow a track to meet a gate, with another gate on your right. Turn right here on a rising path shared with cyclists. Pass through a second gate to meet a third gate at the top of the rise. Follow the signed path to the left for 100 metres, before turning right between fields to meet an unmade lane.

2 Turn left along the lane, which later becomes surfaced and goes uphill to meet a car park. Turn right here, and continue on a rising concrete track. At the top of the rise, with a golf course ahead of you, ignore a stile on your left, and turn left immediately after it on a grassy path with a wire fence on your left. The path ends at a T-junction on the clifftop by an information board.

3 Turn left along the top of the cliff, and follow a wide, grassy path that forms a section of the **Vanguard Way** long-distance path. With fantastic views ahead, the path soon dips into **Hope Gap**.

4 Climb out of **Hope Gap** by keeping to the cliff path, where several well-sited seats offer stunning views of the **Seven Sisters** cliffs. The cliff path ends where it bends left and meets an indistinct cattle grid by a row of clifftop houses.

30

Exceat 9

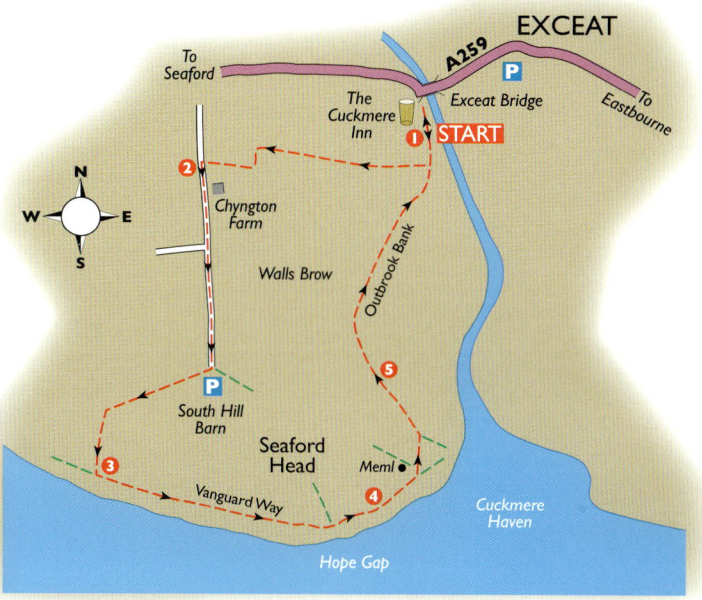

From this cattle grid, and with your back to the sea, cross a grassy area, passing a memorial marking a World War II tragedy. Continue down the slope, and go through a gate in the bottom corner signed '**VGW**' (indicating the Vanguard Way). Keep to this track, later passing through two more pedestrian gates, to eventually return to the pub car park.

PLACES OF INTEREST NEARBY
Seaford Museum of Local History (www.seafordmuseum.co.uk) is run by volunteers, and houses displays that cover Seaford's history as one of the Cinque Ports, as well as many office and domestic items. Check for opening times; you can call on 01323 898222. BN25 1JH.

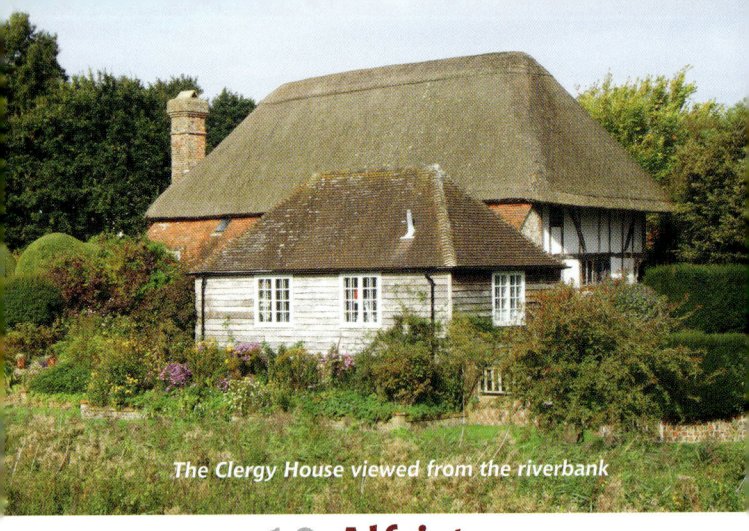
The Clergy House viewed from the riverbank

10 Alfriston
2½ miles (4 km)

WALK HIGHLIGHTS
This short, level route begins in the village centre, which is often described as the jewel in the Sussex crown. The circuit passes by the village green and Alfriston Clergy House to meet the River Cuckmere, where it follows the riverbank south towards Litlington. Here, the way crosses banks then heads back via an easy stroll through scenic fields, leaving plenty of time to explore the captivating village.

THE PUB
The Star Inn, BN26 5TA
☎ 01323 870495   www.thestaralfriston.co.uk.

THE WALK
1 From either car park, walk into the village centre to meet the **Star Inn**. With your back to the inn, cross to the pavement opposite, and turn right. Very soon, go left on a path signed to the **Clergy House**. At the

Alfriston 🔟

HOW TO GET THERE AND PARKING: Alfriston is signed north from the A259 at Seaford or south from the A27 at the Drusillas Park roundabout. Parking at the Star Inn is for residents only, but there are two car parks off North Street just 120 metres northward. On the west side of the street is a free short-stay car park (three hours), and on the east side is a pay and display long-stay car park. Alfriston is a busy tourist spot in the summer, so the car parks may be busy at weekends. **Sat nav** BN26 5UQ.

MAP: OS Explorer OL25 Eastbourne & Beachy Head. **Grid ref** TQ 520031.

village green, fork right to meet the **Clergy House**, where a left turn brings you to a burial ground. Turn immediately right here, and pass through a gap in a hedge. Turn right on a well-trodden path that follows the bank of the **River Cuckmere** for the next 1¼ miles to meet a bridge by **Litlington**.

❷ Turn left over the bridge, and then left again at the far side on a tarmac path. Soon, this path turns right; ignore this turning, and press on ahead on a raised, grassy path alongside the water's edge, passing through some scenic meadows with great views along the way.

33

Guide to East Sussex Pub Walks

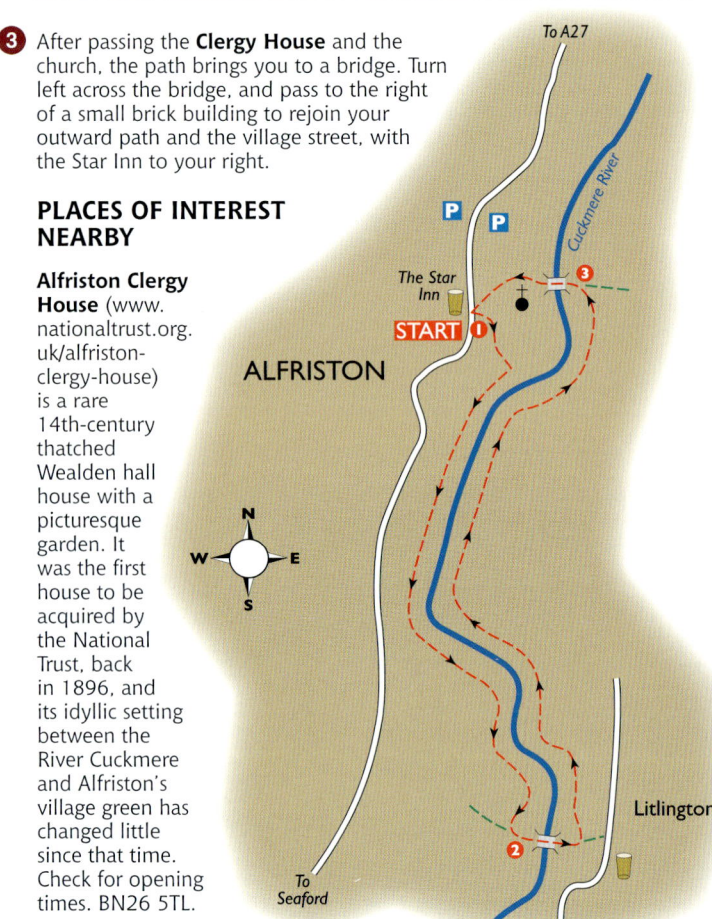

❸ After passing the **Clergy House** and the church, the path brings you to a bridge. Turn left across the bridge, and pass to the right of a small brick building to rejoin your outward path and the village street, with the Star Inn to your right.

PLACES OF INTEREST NEARBY

Alfriston Clergy House (www.nationaltrust.org.uk/alfriston-clergy-house) is a rare 14th-century thatched Wealden hall house with a picturesque garden. It was the first house to be acquired by the National Trust, back in 1896, and its idyllic setting between the River Cuckmere and Alfriston's village green has changed little since that time. Check for opening times. BN26 5TL.

Arlington Reservoir and Nature Reserve

11 Arlington
4¾ miles (7.6 km)

WALK HIGHLIGHTS
This fairly level route leads you across scenic fields, along quiet country lanes and by the water's edge, all set against the backdrop of the magnificent South Downs. The turning point comes when the circuit rounds the Arlington Reservoir, a Site of Special Scientific Interest and a nature reserve. Heading back through the hamlet of Arlington, the route follows a quiet lane as it makes an easy return to the Old Oak Inn.

THE PUB
The Old Oak Inn, BN26 6SJ
☎ 01323 482072   www.oldoakinnarlington.co.uk

THE WALK
1. Facing the pub, pass close to its right side, and cross a stile to enter a field. Go diagonally left to the far right corner. Press on along the right

Guide to East Sussex Pub Walks

HOW TO GET THERE AND PARKING: Arlington is signed west from the A22 near Hailsham between the Eagles and Diplocks Way roundabouts. Pass Arlington Stadium, and turn left at a road junction to meet the pub in ½ mile. Park at the pub with permission, or on the roadside. **Sat nav** BN26 6SJ.

MAP: OS Explorer OL25 Eastbourne & Beachy Head. **Grid ref** TQ 558078.

side of the next field, and maintain the same direction through a third field, crossing a stile in its corner. Turn left alongside a hedgerow, then cross a stile on your right to meet a lane.

2 Turn right along the lane, and at the road junction, go ahead on a narrower lane that soon ends at a farm gate. Go ahead on a narrow byway, later crossing a bridge over the **River Cuckmere**, before meeting a junction of paths by a sign directing you left towards **Arlington Reservoir**.

3 Turn left, and follow the right side of some fields to reach a tree line at the top of a rise. Go ahead on a wide path by some woodland. At a fork, keep left, and follow the path around the water's edge. Later, pass some picnic tables beside a car park and a snack bar. Press on along the waterside path to meet the drive to **Polhill's Farm**.

4 Cross the drive, and continue on a fenced path that skirts the farm to rejoin the driveway at the far side. Turn right on the drive, and soon afterwards, go left through a kissing gate to continue along the service track that tops the reservoir dam.

The Old Oak Inn

5 At the end of the dam,

Arlington 11

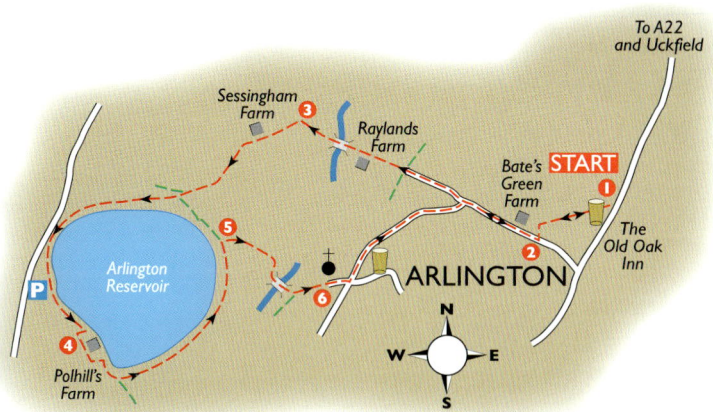

cross a stile to the right of a gate; turn right, and follow a grassy path across a field and pass a marker post. Press on over a planked bridge, and soon afterwards, cross a larger bridge over the River Cuckmere. Turn diagonally left; cross a stile, and go ahead alongside a hedgerow. In 80 metres, go left over a bridge, and cross a field to a stile just left of a house ahead.

Pass the house, and go ahead to meet the **Yew Tree Inn**. Turn left on a lane between the inn and its car park. Keep to the lane to reach a road junction and your outward path. Turn right here; 80 metres after passing **Bate's Green Farm**, go left over a stile, and retrace your earlier steps through three fields to return to the **Old Oak Inn**.

PLACES OF INTEREST NEARBY
Michelham Priory (www.sussexpast.co.uk/properties-to-discover/michelham-priory) is a former Augustinian priory open to the public; the surviving Grade I and Grade II listed buildings are owned by the Sussex Archaeological Society. Follow the brown signs from the A22 at Hailsham. BN27 3QS.

Birling Gap with Seven Sisters cliffs beyond

12 East Dean

3¼ miles (5.2 km)

WALK HIGHLIGHTS
This super walk begins at the scenic village green that fronts the Tiger Inn. Soon after leaving the pub, the route makes a short climb to the top of the Seven Sisters Country Park, where the views are stunning. Descending into Birling Gap, the circuit skirts a cliff topped by Belle Tout Lighthouse to meet the turning point, where an easy stroll through rolling farmland returns you to the village.

THE PUB
The Tiger Inn, BN20 0DA
☎ 01323 423209 www.beachyhead.org.uk/the-tiger-inn

THE WALK
1 From the car park, walk away from the road to meet the village green and the **Tiger Inn**. Turn left, and with your back to the pub, go ahead

East Dean

HOW TO GET THERE AND PARKING: East Dean is just south of the A259, 2½ miles west of Eastbourne. A couple of hundred metres after leaving the A259, turn right into Village Green Lane for the car park. There is no parking available at the pub itself. **Sat nav** BN20 0DL.

MAP: OS Explorer OL11 Brighton & Hove. **Grid ref** TV 557978.

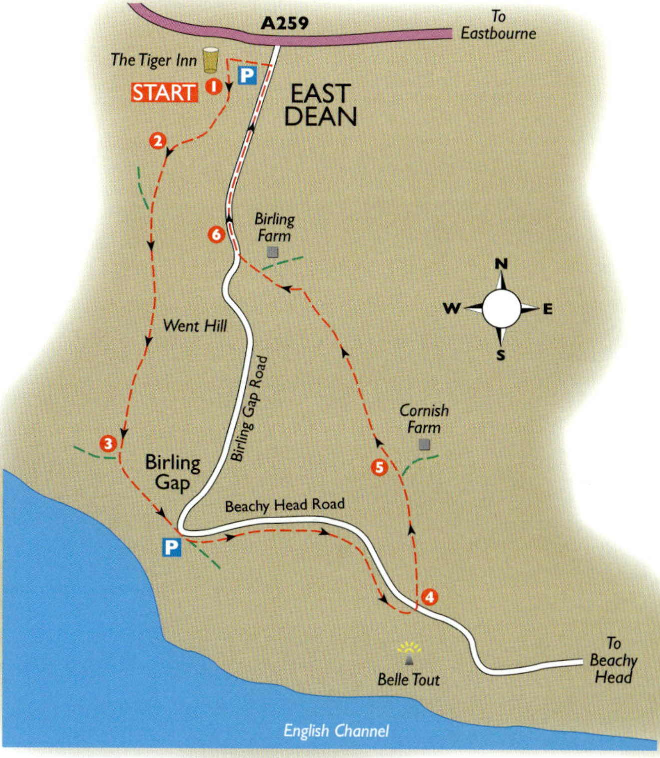

Guide to East Sussex Pub Walks

along the left side of the green to meet a lane. Go diagonally left, and continue along **Went Way**.

2 At the road's end, go through a gate, and follow a path uphill through woodland to reach open downs. Press on ahead, and pass an isolated barn. Keep ahead, aiming just to the right of a house in the distance. Pass through two pedestrian gates to meet a rough track by the house.

3 Follow the track left and downhill to meet the car parks and café at **Birling Gap**, where the more adventurous can descend the steps to the beach. The route continues ahead through a car park beside a telephone box. Avoid the steep uphill path, and go to the end of the car park beside the road, before continuing along a well-trodden path that skirts the foot of the hill.

4 After passing through woodland, the path crosses open downland, where you should look out for the concrete drive to **Cornish Farm** across the road to your left. Now follow this drive until it bends right to the farm.

5 Leave the drive here by continuing ahead alongside a couple of large fields until you meet a gate. Go ahead on a curving path lined by trees and continue along the drive of **Birling Farm** to join **Birling Gap Road**.

6 Press on ahead on a wide grassy strip beside the road; pass the village cricket pitch and some houses to return to the car park and the Tiger Inn.

PLACES OF INTEREST NEARBY
Beachy Head Countryside & Visitor Centre (www.beachyhead.org) is located further along Beachy Head Road, and is close to the famous, dramatic clifftop that forms the eastern gateway to the South Downs National Park. The exhibits describe the flora and fauna of the downland, as well as the feat of building the Beachy Head Lighthouse below the cliffs. BN20 7YA.

Scenic fields are a feature of the route

13 Mayfield
3¼ miles (5.2 km)

WALK HIGHLIGHTS
This gloriously varied route leaves the historic village via the extensive grounds of a girls' boarding school, before following quiet farm lanes and field paths through a picturesque setting. Between the fields are areas of peaceful woodland where the only sound to break the silence is birdsong. All in all, this is a lovely rural walk, with a good pub and an interesting village to explore at its end.

THE PUB
The Middle House Hotel, TN20 6AB
☎ 01435 872146   www.themiddlehousemayfield.co.uk

THE WALK

1 From the pub, cross the road, and turn left along the pavement, passing the church. Turn right between shops on an alley called **North Street**. At **Foxglove Cottage**, continue between hedgerows to reach and pass through a gate, entering some school grounds. Bear left, before turning right and walking along the rear of some tennis courts with a hedgerow to your left. Now follow the side of this hedgerow through fields, until it finally bends right in the last field to bring you to a gate and a road.

2 Turn left along the road, and in 50 metres, go right along a short road that ends at some posts. Go ahead on a bridleway; finally, this passes under a bridge, where it turns sharp right to meet a quiet lane. Turn

Guide to East Sussex Pub Walks

HOW TO GET THERE AND PARKING: Mayfield is signed off the A267, 5 miles north of Heathfield. The pub is in the High Street. There is parking at the pub for customers; you can also park alongside the High Street or in the free village car park, which is signed 50 metres east of the pub. **Sat nav** TN20 6AB.

MAP: OS Explorer 135 Ashdown Forest. **Grid ref** TQ 587270.

left along the lane, which eventually becomes the driveway to **Great Trodgers Farm**.

❸ At a sharp left bend, turn right over a stile into a field. Go ahead, and at the top of a rise, ignore a gate on your right, and continue ahead along the field edge to meet and pass through a gate in the bottom corner. Press on through woodland to meet and cross a stile and enter a field. Now go ahead along the right-hand edges of this field and the next.

❹ On a downward slope, turn right over a stile, and enter woodland. Go ahead alongside a field boundary, and at a field gate, follow the path left to reach a road. Turn right along the road, and in 80 metres, turn left on a signed path along the drive of **Old Place Cottage**.

❺ At a house named **The Stables**, go ahead on a grassy path, and pass through a gate. Keep ahead through woodland and a second gate, and go ahead to the end of a field. Go through a gate here, and turn immediately right on a path through woodland to reach another field. Go ahead uphill towards a tree line, which the path soon follows. At the top of the rise, press on along the well-trodden path, and pass by a house to meet a junction of paths.

❻ Turn right here; soon afterwards, go over two stiles to meet a crossing track. Go ahead up some steps to enter a recreation ground. Continue along its right side, and pass **Mayfield Memorial Hall** to reach a road, where a left turn brings you back to the **High Street** and the pub.

PLACES OF INTEREST NEARBY
Pashley Manor Gardens (www.pashleymanorgardens.com) has an award-winning display of superb trees, artistic plantings and large

Mayfield 13

ponds, all set in an exquisite English landscaped setting. Open April to September (not Sundays or Mondays). TN5 7HE.

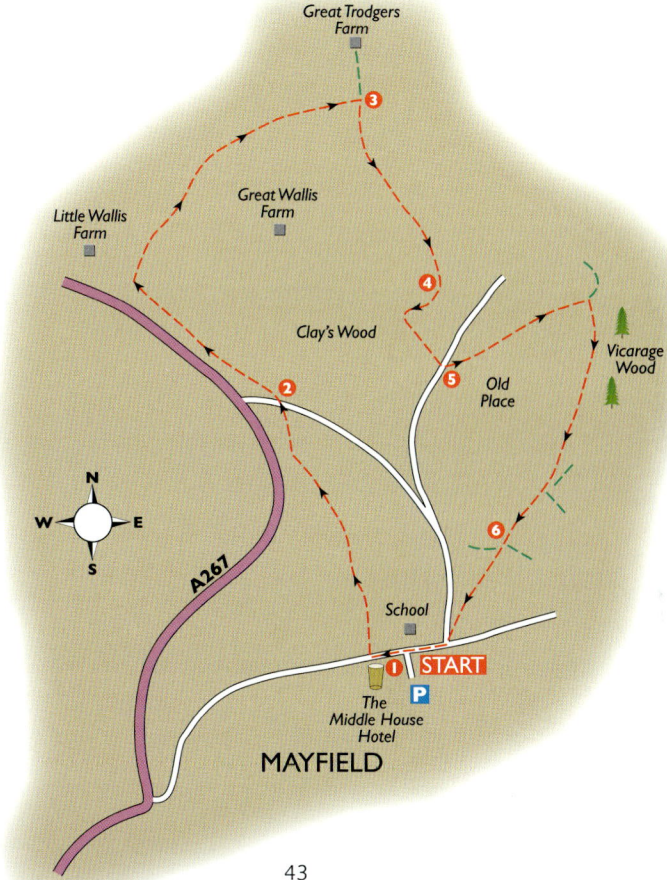

Warbleton church across the fields

14 Rushlake Green
4¾ miles (7.6 km)

WALK HIGHLIGHTS
This lovely walk takes in three small Sussex villages, each one with an enticing pub – so thirst should not be a problem on a hot day. Beginning in pretty Rushlake Green, the route crosses scenic fields, with wonderful views across the High Weald. This area of rolling countryside has long been designated as an Area of Outstanding Natural Beauty – an attribute confirmed with each field path walked.

THE PUB
Horse & Groom, TN21 9QE
☎ 01435 830320 www.horseandgroomsussex.co.uk

Rushlake Green 14

HOW TO GET THERE AND PARKING: Rushlake Green is signed off the B2096 at Three Cups Corner, three miles south-east of Heathfield. The pub faces the green. There is parking at the pub for customers or by the roadside around the green. **Sat nav** TN21 9QE.

MAP: OS Explorer OL25 Eastbourne & Beachy Head. **Grid ref** TQ 626184.

THE WALK

Facing the pub, turn right, and seek out a narrow footpath between the first two houses. The footpath sign is low and is easily missed! Press on between the paddocks, before continuing through woodland on a well-trodden path. After exiting the woodland, go ahead over a field, and pass a direction post. Later, ignore a path forking right, and keep ahead to reach a lane.

Cross the lane, and continue on a bridleway opposite. Keep to the well-defined bridleway to reach a road. Turn left along the road, and in 70 metres, cross a hidden stile on top of the bank to your right. Go diagonally left on a grassy path, and cross a stile in the far corner of the field, under the power cables.

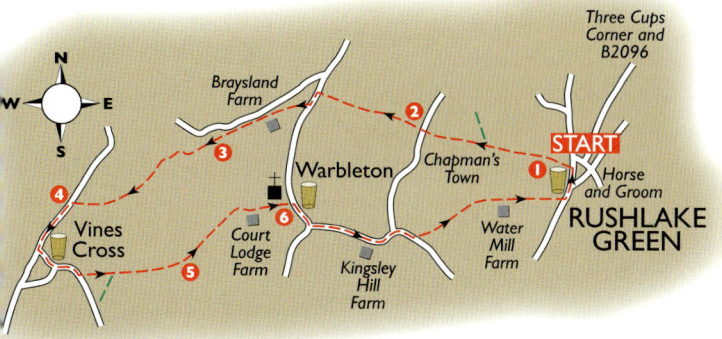

45

Guide to East Sussex Pub Walks

3 Now turn right, follow the field edge to its end, and cross a stile in a hedgerow. Go ahead – you soon have a hedgerow on your right – and just before a house is met, follow the path to the right. Pass a direction post, and turn left alongside a meadow and under some power cables. At the meadow's end, cross a bridge and then a stile before forking left, with a hedgerow on your right. Pass through a field gate on your right, and follow a cart track to meet a drive, which leads to a road.

4 Turn left along the road, and enter the village of **Vines Cross**. Immediately after passing the **Brewers Arms** pub, turn left along **Foords Lane**. Soon after passing the last house on your left, ignore a signed footpath to the left, and 30 metres further on, turn left over a stile. Turn right, and keep to the field edge as it remains parallel with the road, before soon turning rightwards in its corner. Press on along the right field edge, and at a second field, continue along its left edge before passing through the centre of a large field on a well-trodden path.

5 At the far side, cross a footbridge, and continue ahead, now with a hedgerow on your right. Maintain the same direction alongside the next field to meet a marker post opposite **St Mary's Church**, which is atop **Church Hill**, on your right. Turn right here over the field to reach the graveyard and a curious memorial in the wall. Pass to the right of the church to meet the road in the hamlet of **Warbleton**.

6 Turn right, pass the **Black Duck** pub, and at a road junction, turn left along **Kingsley Hill**. After a climb, ignore a road on your left, and on the downward slope, turn left on a signed footpath opposite **Kingsley Hill Farm**. The path passes through woodland and ends back at **Rushlake Green**.

PLACES OF INTEREST NEARBY
The Observatory Science Centre (www.the-observatory.org) is 5 miles south of Rushlake Green. The centre promises visitors a 'spectacular hands-on science and discovery experience among the domes and telescopes of a world-famous astronomical observatory'. Just east of Windmill Hill on the A271, go south on Wartling Road to meet the centre. (The official postcode will misdirect you.)

Bewl Water

15 Wadhurst

4¼ miles (6.8 km)

WALK HIGHLIGHTS
This route passes through some of the finest rural scenery on offer in southern England. Within metres of the pub door, the undulating circuit immerses itself in a countryside idyll, and is soon passing hop fields on its way to the banks of Bewl Water, the largest body of inland water in the South-East. Turning back towards Wadhurst, the route crosses rolling fields with outstanding views.

THE PUB
The Greyhound Inn, TN5 6AP
☎ 01892 783224 www.thegreyhoundwadhurst.co.uk

Guide to East Sussex Pub Walks

HOW TO GET THERE AND PARKING: Wadhurst sits on the B2099, 7 miles south of Royal Tunbridge Wells. The pub is at the eastern end of the High Street. There is a large free car park beside the pub. **Sat nav** TN5 6AP.

MAP: OS Explorer 136 High Weald. **Grid ref** TQ 641317.

THE WALK

1 With your back to the pub, cross the **High Street**, and go along **Blacksmith's Lane** opposite. Soon, the lane bends sharp left; do not follow the bend, but instead go ahead along the drive to **Little Pell Farm**. Pass the farmhouse and the large barns, and press on along a track.

2 When you meet two field gates, cross a stile beside the left-hand gate, and continue along the track. When the track turns left into fields, go ahead along a ribbon of woodland before crossing a stile and entering a field.

3 Go ahead to the left corner of the field, and cross a stile to meet a bridleway. Turn right, and follow the bridleway, which skirts the initially unseen **Bewl Water**.

4 Eventually, the bridleway meets a brown **Bewl Water Route** sign. Turn right uphill here, and follow the path, which soon meets a private road. Turn right along the road to meet a T-junction with a quiet lane. Turn right along the lane.

5 Soon after passing the entrance to **Chesson's Farm**, and just before a left bend, turn right through a gate on a signed footpath. Go down the right side of a field to meet a marker post between two large oak trees. Turn left on the path; you will soon pass between banks, before the path bends right to meet a gate. Pass through the gate, and follow the grassy path, with a fence to your left.

6 The path continues uphill towards some buildings, where you should pass through a gate just to the right of a cottage to meet a drive. Turn left along the drive. Just after passing the entrance to **Laundry Cottage**, turn right down some steps and through a kissing gate.

Wadhurst 15

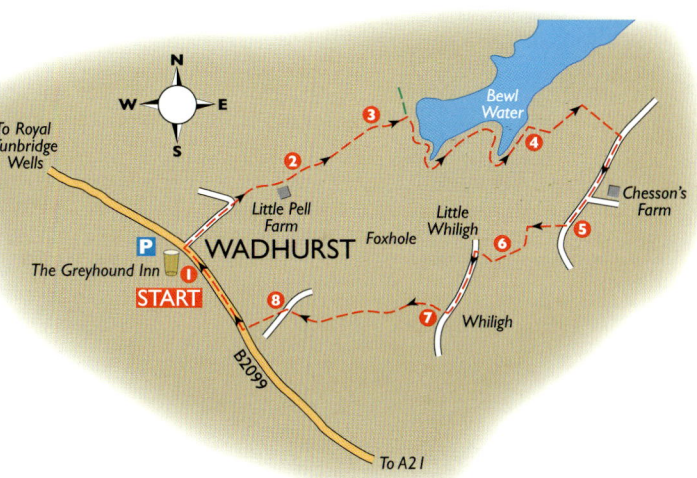

7 Go ahead along the field boundary; the grassy path bends left and meets a stile at the woodland's edge. Cross the stile, and pass through the woodland and over a bridge. Bear slightly right, enter a field, and follow its left boundary uphill to meet **Foxhole Lane**.

8 Cross the lane, enter a field, and now follow a path diagonally left to the field corner. Cross a stile to meet the B2099. Turn right here along the pavement for an easy stroll to return to the pub.

PLACES OF INTEREST NEARBY
Scotney Castle (www.nationaltrust.org.uk/scotney-castle) is 5 miles north-east of Wadhurst. The typically English country house is set in formal gardens, within which are the ruins of a medieval moated manor house, set on an island. Open all year. TN3 8JN.

Bateman's – once the home of Rudyard Kipling

16 Burwash
5 miles (8 km)

WALK HIGHLIGHTS
This super field and woodland route leads you through an unsurpassed Wealden landscape, where a backdrop of outstanding views will be enjoyed for almost the entire route. The circuit passes Bateman's, once the home of Rudyard Kipling, before it continues through peaceful woodland and undulating fields as it passes Franchise Manor to return to Burwash.

THE PUB
The Bear Inn, TN19 7ET
☎ 01435 882540 www.bear-inn-hotel-burwash.co.uk

THE WALK

1 From the free car park, with your back to the road, follow a path in the left corner to meet a field. Go ahead to meet a directional post. Turn right here; cross a bridge, pass through a gate, and go ahead to meet and pass through a second gate. Press on along the field edge, and pass through a gate at its end.

2 Continue diagonally left on the grassy path, and remain on it as it curves right around a pond. Pass through a gap in the hedgerow at the bottom corner of the pond, and turn left along the field edge. Cross a stile in the bottom corner to meet a country lane. Turn right along the lane; very soon, you will meet with **Bateman's**.

Burwash 16

HOW TO GET THERE AND PARKING: Burwash is on the A265, 6 miles east of Heathfield. The pub is at the western end of the High Street. Use the adjoining free village car park. **Sat nav** TN19 7ET.

MAP: OS Explorer 136 High Weald. **Grid ref** TQ 673246.

3 Turn left along a drive to reach **Corner Cottage** on your right. Turn right here on a cart track, and pass between an old watermill and a millpond. Continue along the path, and pass through a gate to enter woodland. Soon, at a directional post, ignore a path and a bridge on your right, and keep ahead. Continue ahead on a grassy path along the left side of a meadow to meet a field gate on your left at its end.

Guide to East Sussex Pub Walks

4 Pass through the gate, and turn right alongside the field edge. At the field end, ignore a path on your left, and continue ahead alongside the next meadow. In 120 metres, when you are beside an oak tree, turn right over a bridge before turning left along the field edge, and pass through a kissing gate to follow a path through **Bog Wood**.

5 At a gate, enter a paddock. Go uphill to meet a fence, and turn left alongside it. Go right through a kissing gate, and after a second gate, go diagonally right to a driveway between a couple of houses, which you should follow to reach the A265 road.

6 Using caution, cross the road, and turn right alongside it. In 40 metres, turn left onto a stony track; very soon, the track forks. Take the right fork; pass the side of a house, and follow this scenic bridleway for 1¼ miles.

7 At a country lane, turn left, and in 40 metres, turn right along the drive to **Franchise Manor**. 30 metres before meeting some large gates, cross a stile on your right, and maintain your original direction along the left side of a field. Go through a kissing gate at the far end, continue ahead through a second kissing gate, and press on ahead.

8 At the end of this field, pass through a gap in the hedgerow, and turn right along the field edge to meet and cross a stile beside a cattle grid. After this, the path forks. Follow the left fork across a field; pass through a gate, and continue on a well-trodden path through woodland.

9 Exit the woodland, and continue diagonally right on a grassy path to the top corner of the field, where you will meet a farm drive. Turn right along the drive, which leads you back to the **High Street** in **Burwash**; here, a right turn brings you to the **Bear Inn**.

PLACES OF INTEREST NEARBY

Bateman's (www.nationaltrust.org.uk/batemans) is a Jacobean house built for John Brittan, a wealthy local ironmaster during the 17th century. It is famous today as the former home of Rudyard Kipling, author of many books. TN19 7DS

Battle Great Wood

17 Battle
4¾ miles (7.6 km)

WALK HIGHLIGHTS
This undulating route leads you away from the bustling High Street to meet Battle Great Wood, one of the last vestiges of the large forest that covered most of East Sussex during the 10th and 11th centuries. The mix of trees is a delight, and the wide rides through the woodland, with its plentiful wildlife, are a joy to explore – as is quaint Battle High Street, on your return.

THE PUB
The Bull Inn, TN33 0EA
☎ 01424 775171 www.thebullinnbattle.co.uk

Guide to East Sussex Pub Walks

HOW TO GET THERE AND PARKING: Battle is on the A2100, 5 miles north-west of Hastings. The pub is towards the northern end of the High Street. There is no parking at the pub itself, but there is some free parking alongside the High Street. Behind the shops opposite the pub is a pay and display car park, which is reached via Mount Street, a few metres north of the pub. There is an alley leading from the car park back to the High Street. **Sat nav** TN33 0EA.

MAP: OS Explorer 124 Hastings & Bexhill. **Grid ref** TQ 746159.

THE WALK

1 From the **Bull Inn**, cross the road; turn right down the **High Street**, and in 60 metres, go left on an alley between shops to meet the **Mount Street** car park. Go ahead through the car park, passing a public convenience, and enter the overflow car park. Turn immediately left here to meet a lane. Go right down the lane.

2 At the foot of a slope, with a house ahead and footpaths signed to left and right, go right on a well-trodden path. The path leads through a series of small meadows to reach a railway bridge. Go under the bridge to meet a water treatment works, turn left, and after 10 metres, turn right alongside the works fence.

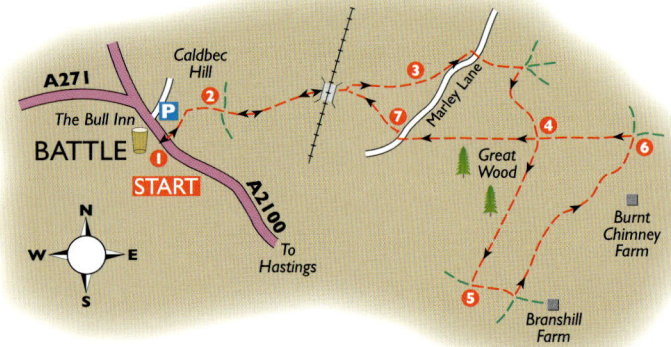

Battle

At a field, go ahead to the right of a barn to meet **Marley Lane**. Turn left along the road; you will soon reach **Battle Great Wood** car park. Turn right through the car park, and enter the woodland on a track. When you reach a broad track on your right, turn right and follow it as it slowly rises.

Ignore a wide crossing track, and press on ahead. At the top of the rise, ignore a left fork, and keep ahead. Later, as the track bends right at the top of another rise, keep ahead on a wide, rising, grassy ride, and press on to meet a T-junction at a tree line in the distance.

Turn left here on a grassy path to meet a second T-junction. Now turn left, and continue on a grassy ride that gradually loses height. On the way down the slope, ignore a right fork, and keep to the main track.

At a wide crossing track, with a seat to your right, turn left and follow this straight track, which crosses your outward path along the way. Finally, the track narrows, passes a house and ends at **Marley Lane**.

Cross to the verge opposite, and turn right to meet a concrete drive in 60 metres. Go left along the drive; at its end, ignore a path signed left, and instead fork left to return to the railway bridge. Pass under the bridge, and continue on the path through the small meadows as you retrace your footsteps back to the pub.

The Bull Inn

PLACES OF INTEREST NEARBY
Battle Abbey (www.english-heritage.org.uk) is just down the High Street from the pub. It was built on the site of the Battle of Hastings, and is an interesting place to visit. TN33 0AD.

The fine old barn at Great Dixter

18 Ewhurst Green

4½ miles (7.2 km)

WALK HIGHLIGHTS
Within metres of leaving the pub, this great field walk passes through unrivalled pastoral scenery. The lightly undulating route, which is easy to follow, leaves Ewhurst Green along wonderful field paths as it heads towards Northiam, where it passes Lutyens' Great Dixter. The return route continues through scenic fields before rejoining the outward path to complete the circuit.

THE PUB
The White Dog Inn, TN32 5TD
☎ 01580 830264 www.thewhitedogewhurst.co.uk.

Ewhurst Green 18

HOW TO GET THERE AND PARKING: From the A21, south of Hurst Green, follow signs to Bodiam Castle. Pass the castle, and in ½ mile, turn left along Dagg Lane. At a T-junction, turn left to meet the village street; the pub is towards its far end. Park at the pub with permission or considerately at the roadside. **Sat nav** TN32 5TD.

MAP: OS Explorers 136 High Weald and 125 Romney Marsh, Rye & Winchelsea. **Grid ref** TQ 795246.

THE WALK

1. With your back to the pub, go left along the road. In 85 metres, go right over a stile, and continue alongside a hedgerow. When you meet a signed path, turn left through the hedgerow, ignore a path on your right, and go ahead alongside a large field to its end.

2. Turn right over a wooden bridge, and follow the field edge to reach some power cables. Turn left over a stile, and then turn right along a lane to meet and cross a stile on your left in 130 metres. Follow the right-hand field edge to meet a wooden bridge at its end. Cross the bridge, and go diagonally left across a field on a path to meet a wooden bridge at the far side.

3. Do not cross this bridge. Turn right along the field edge to meet a marker post in the corner, and go through the woodland to a field. Go ahead on a path through the centre of the field. At the far side, cross a bridge, go through a kissing gate, and continue along the left side of the next field.

4. Look out for a signed path on your left; here, you should go left through the hedgerow before turning right alongside the next field, which ends at a country lane. Cross the lane to the drive of **Strawberry Hole**, and go left on a fenced path to pass a cottage.

5. At a field, go ahead to a marker post. Pass a second post, and go through a gap in the hedge ahead to meet a finger post. Ignore the right-hand path, and continue ahead through a field until you reach its end. Now press on alongside a recreation ground to meet the main street in **Northiam**.

Guide to East Sussex Pub Walks

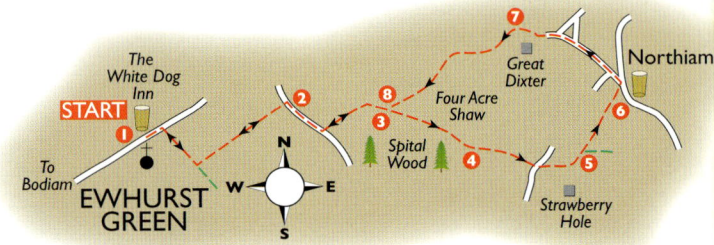

6 Turn left along the road, and soon fork left along a residential road. Continue to its far end, following the brown signs to **Great Dixter**. At the entrance to Great Dixter, go ahead on a narrow path alongside the drive to reach a parking area.

7 Go ahead, and pass through a kissing gate to the left of a cattle grid. Follow the signed path ahead to meet a large field. Follow the left edge of the field, and pass through a kissing gate at its end. Go diagonally right through the next field towards a large oak tree. Continue through a kissing gate in the left corner, and press on ahead at the next field. At the field end, cross a bridge to rejoin your outward path.

8 Go diagonally right across the field to a finger post, and cross the bridge. Turn left along the field edge to meet the lane. Turn right, and in 130 metres, go left over the stile. Turn right along the field edge, and cross a wooden bridge in the corner. Turn left along the next field, and at its end, pass through a hedgerow. Turn right on the rising path to meet the road and the pub.

PLACES OF INTEREST NEARBY
Bodiam Castle (www.nationaltrust.org.uk/bodiam-castle) is a 14th-century moated castle, built as part of the defences against French invasion during the Hundred Years War. The castle is 1¾ miles north of Ewhurst Green. TN32 5UA.

The peace and tranquillity of the Royal Military Canal

19 Winchelsea
2½ miles (4 km)

WALK HIGHLIGHTS
This varied route begins in the heart of the ancient town, and soon passes under the medieval Strand Gate to join the Royal Military Canal below. Here, a lovely path is followed alongside the tranquil waters, before the way turns across a field to meet a quiet lane. Heading back, the way passes under 13th-century New Gate on its easy return to the town.

THE PUB
The New Inn, TN36 4EN
☎ 01797 226252 www.newinnpubwinchelsea.co.uk

THE WALK
1 With your back to the pub, go ahead along the **High Street**, with the museum on your left and a churchyard on your right. At the far end of the street, go left down the steps, and pass by the ancient **Strand Gate** that once protected the town. Now go ahead downhill to a road junction.

Guide to East Sussex Pub Walks

HOW TO GET THERE AND PARKING: Winchelsea is off the A259, 2 miles west of Rye. The pub is on the corner of German Street and High Street, opposite the church of St Thomas the Martyr. There is parking at the pub for customers, and plenty of free roadside parking. **Sat nav** TN36 4EN.

MAP: OS Explorer 125 Romney Marsh, Rye & Winchelsea. **Grid ref** TQ 904174.

2 The route here is rightwards alongside the road, but for safety's sake, it is better to cross the road to the pavement opposite before returning to this side in 80 metres. Very soon, turn right into **Sea Road**, and in 60 metres, go right through a pedestrian gate. Now follow this lovely canal-side path for a mile, until you meet a bridge.

3 Turn right over the bridge, and go ahead towards the woodland. Skirt around the trees, and pass through a gate to meet a country lane. Turn right along the lane, soon passing under **New Gate**, another ancient town defence. Remain on this lovely lane, which offers fantastic views, until you meet a road junction. Here, go ahead alongside a low parkland wall to eventually return to the **New Inn**.

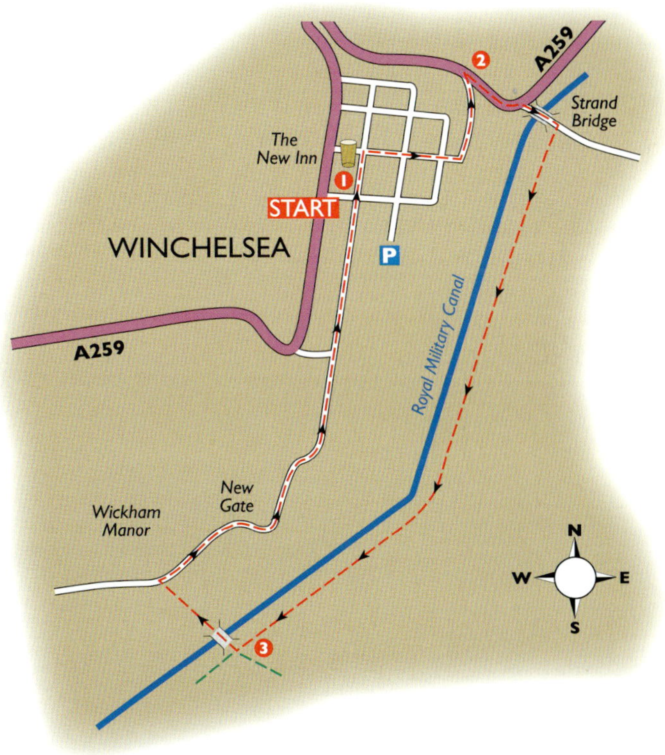

Winchelsea

PLACES OF INTEREST NEARBY
Court Hall Museum (www.winchelsea.com/museum/visit-us) is just a few metres from the pub and is one of the oldest buildings in the town. It houses displays illustrating the history and daily life of the area. Exhibits include maps, models and local pottery. TN36 4EA.

Rye Harbour beach

20 Rye Harbour
4¼ miles (6.8 km) or 7¼ miles (11.7 km)

WALK HIGHLIGHTS
This good, flat walk leaves Rye Harbour via a wonderful track through Rye Harbour Nature Reserve. As the route approaches Winchelsea Beach, the longer circuit heads inland to meet Camber Castle before turning back towards the sea; here, depending on the tides, both routes give the opportunity of walking barefoot along the sands of the generally deserted beach.

THE PUB
William the Conqueror, TN31 7TU
☎ 01797 223315 www.williamtheconqueror.co.uk

❶ THE WALK
From the pub, walk back to the public conveniences. Turn right along **Harbour Road**, and 60 metres after passing the **Inkerman Arms** pub, go left into **Oyster Creek**. Where this short lane ends, go through a gate, and follow a wide track through the nature reserve for 1½ miles.

Rye Harbour

HOW TO GET THERE AND PARKING: Just west of Rye town, turn off the A259 where signed to Rye Harbour. The road ends after 2 miles at a large free car park and public conveniences. The pub is 100 metres along the lane to the left. **Sat nav** TN31 7TU.

MAP: OS Explorer 125 Romney Marsh, Rye & Winchelsea. **Grid ref** TQ 942191.

The track finally meets a junction of paths by a seat, with a garden beyond. **The shorter walk** *turns left here. Follow the route from Point 7.* **For the longer route,** turn right by a marker post on a path that soon goes through woodland and ends at a track. Turn right for 10 metres before turning left over a stile. Follow a path, and cross a bridge ahead; then go half-left through the next field, and pass through a gate. Go ahead, and cross a bridge and a stile to reach a farm drive.

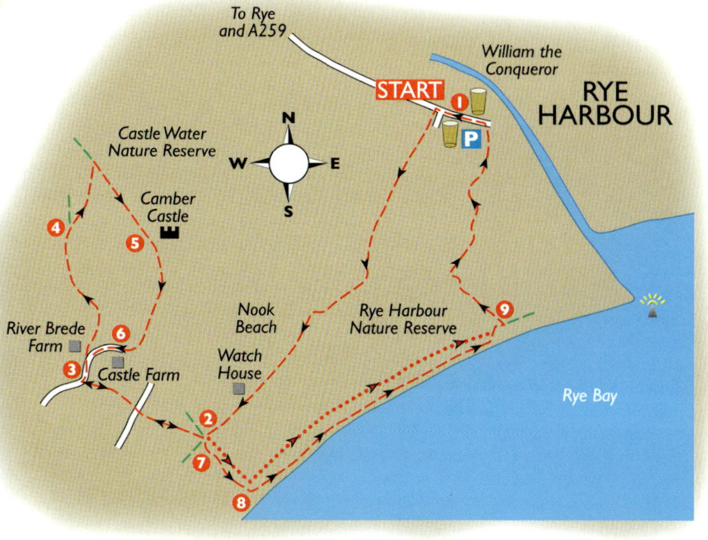

Guide to East Sussex Pub Walks

3 Turn right along the drive, and at a bend, go through the gate to **River Brede Farm** on a bridleway. Where the drive ends, go through a gate, and continue on a raised path. Remain on this path, which has views to **Camber Castle**.

4 Opposite the castle, bear right on a raised path to meet a marker post beside an odd concrete structure. Turn sharply right through a gate on a signed footpath towards the castle.

5 Pass the castle, go through a gate, and follow a track through a large field. At the field end, pass through a gate, and go right along a track. Pass buildings and a gate by cottages to the farm drive you walked earlier.

6 Soon, go left over the stile, and follow the path through the fields walked earlier to reach the track. Turn right for 10 metres, before going left along your outward path to return to the junction of paths by the seat.

7 Follow a path seaward beside a large concrete block to reach an **Environment Agency** track. Go ahead across a shingle bank, and turn left along the beach. ***If the tide is tight to the shingle bank, go left along the Environment Agency track.***

8 Walk along the sands for 1¼ miles before climbing the shingle bank by the last two groynes to rejoin the track. Turn right to meet a path on your left by an information board and a seat. (If you have been walking along the track, these will be on your left.)

9 Follow this path back through the nature reserve; it passes a holiday caravan site and ends at a wide track, where a left turn brings you back to the car park and the pub.

PLACES OF INTEREST NEARBY
Ypres Tower, also known as **Rye Castle** (www.ryemuseum.co.uk), can be found in the centre of Rye, 2 miles inland from Rye Harbour. It was built in 1249 to protect Rye from frequent French raids. TN31 7HE.